Teens in Spain

Spain

BY Jason Skog

Content Adviser: María del Mar Gómez, M.A.
Assistant Professor,
New York University in Madrid

Reading Adviser: Peggy Ballard, Ph.D.,
Department of Educational Studies,
Minnesota State University, Mankato

Compass Point Books ✦ Minneapolis, Minnesota

Compass Point Books
3109 West 50th Street, #115
Minneapolis, MN 55410

Editor: Shelly Lyons
Designers: The Design Lab and Jaime Martens
Page Production: The Design Lab and Ashlee Schultz
Photo Researcher: The Design Lab
Cartographer: XNR Productions, Inc.
Library Consultant: Kathleen Baxter

Art Director: Jaime Martens
Creative Director: Keith Griffin
Editorial Director: Carol Jones
Managing Editor: Catherine Neitge

Library of Congress Cataloging-in-Publication Data
Skog, Jason.
Teens in Spain / by Jason Skog.
    p. cm.—(Global connections)
  Includes bibliographical references and index.
  ISBN-13: 978-0-7565-2446-3 (library binding)
  ISBN-10: 0-7565-2446-6 (library binding)
  1. Teenagers—Spain—Social conditions—Juvenile literature. 2. Teenagers—Spain—Social
life and customs—Juvenile literature. I. Title. II. Series.
  HQ799.S7S57 2007
  305.2350946—dc22   2006027063

Visit Compass Point Books on the Internet at www.compasspointbooks.com
    or e-mail your request to custserv@compasspointbooks.com

Table of Contents

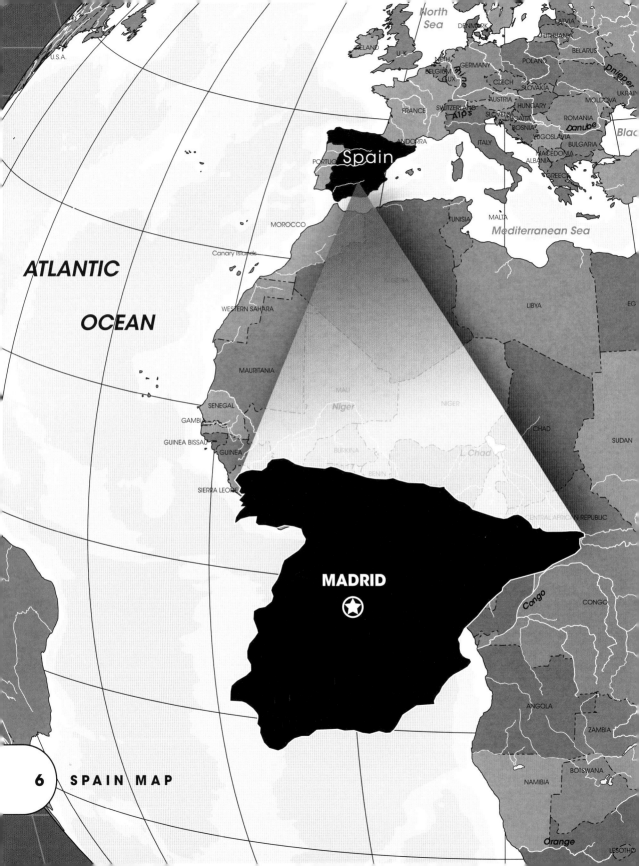

Volga
Irtysh
MONGOLIA
L. Balkhash
KAZAKHSTAN
RUSSIA
KYRGYZSTAN
UZBEKISTAN
CHINA
Sea
GEORGIA
TAJIKISTAN
AZERBAIJAN
ARMENIA
TURKMENISTAN
Caspian Sea
TURKEY
AFGHANISTAN
SYRIA
IRAQ
BHUTAN
Euphrates
IRAN
NEPAL
ISRAEL
Indus
BANGLADESH
JORDAN
KUWAIT
Ganges
PAKISTAN
OMAN
Bay
of
Bengal
QATAR
INDIA
U.A.E.
OMAN
SAUDI ARABIA
Arabian Sea
Red Sea
YEMEN
Nile
ERITREA
DJIBOUTI
SRI LANKA
SOMALIA
ETHIOPIA
INDIAN
OCEAN
UGANDA
KENYA
L. Victoria
TANZANIA
L. Malawi
MALAWI
MOZAMBIQUE
MADAGASCAR
SWAZILAND

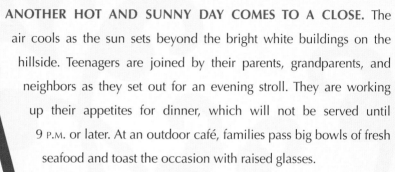

ANOTHER HOT AND SUNNY DAY COMES TO A CLOSE. The air cools as the sun sets beyond the bright white buildings on the hillside. Teenagers are joined by their parents, grandparents, and neighbors as they set out for an evening stroll. They are working up their appetites for dinner, which will not be served until 9 P.M. or later. At an outdoor café, families pass big bowls of fresh seafood and toast the occasion with raised glasses.

Similar scenes unfold each evening in small villages, rural towns, and central squares of cities throughout Spain. Still, the experiences of teenagers, who make up just 10 percent of the population in Spain, can vary greatly in a country that has crowded and busy cities, lush and peaceful farmland, and warm and relaxing beaches.

While people ages 10 to 19 years old make up a minority of the country's population, their influence is strong. Whether Spanish teens struggle with school, opt for a technical education, or press on with college, they are a key part of the future of Spain.

Recent statistics show that around 62 percent of Spain's students finish high school.

CHAPTER ONE

Going Through the Ciclos

IT WAS NOT UNTIL 1970 that Spanish children were required to attend school. Now they must be enrolled from ages 6 to 16.

Public school is free, but parents usually pay for books, supplies, and after-school activities like sports, community plays, or youth clubs. Parents also pay for clothing or uniforms. Most private school students wear uniforms that are chosen by the individual schools—most of which are run by the Roman Catholic Church. White shirts are the most common choice for school uniforms because they reflect the sun's intense heat and help keep students cool.

Around 30 percent of schools in Spain are concertados, which are private schools that receive funding

concertados
con-sir-TAH-dos

Francisco Franco

Francisco Franco ruled Spain from the end of the Spanish Civil War in 1939 to the time of his death in 1975. Although he helped to end much political and social disorder within Spain, he also was responsible for creating a political system in which citizens' rights and freedoms were ignored. Franco also established harsh punishments for anyone who opposed his regime.

In 1969, Franco declared that Don Juan Carlos de Borbón, the grandson of Spain's former king Alfonso XIII, would take over as his successor. After Franco's death in 1975, King Juan Carlos began working toward transitioning his country to a democracy.

from both the government and private organizations. Most of the concertados are owned by sectors of the Catholic Church. The concertados are controversial, because they are able to operate under some of their own rules, such as

refusing to admit children who have behavioral issues, or children who are immigrants. Public schools are not able to do this, and they must operate only with the funds they receive from the government.

The vast majority of students move on to the next grade, but more than 26 percent of all 14-year-olds repeat a grade.

Almost all schools are co-educational, with boys and girls in classrooms together. In larger cities and towns, more than 90 percent of the children go to nursery school or preschool before starting kindergarten.

A typical school year has three 11-week terms. The academic year in Spain runs from mid-September until mid-June. Individual regions establish the specific dates.

During the year, there are two long breaks: December 23 to January 8 and spring break from April 3 to April 13. Summer recess runs from June 20 to September 5. Schools are also closed during public holidays or during local festivals.

Students finishing elementary school have an extra two weeks of break before starting middle school. That time often includes an end-of-school trip with classmates to the beach or inland to the mountains for camping and scavenger hunts.

A Typical School Day in Spain

For most Spanish students, the day begins with breakfast at home and a walk to school. Some students get a ride from their parents or take public transportation because school buses are uncommon, especially in large cities. Some private schools offer school buses, but only for those students who live far away from school. Although many Spanish families own cars, teens are still regular riders of the RENFE, a national network of government-owned trains

Many teens rely on public transportation to get to and from school.

that span much of the country.

Most classes begin at about 9 A.M. Class periods last about 45 minutes, allowing time for students to move between classrooms before beginning the next period. Students who live close to school sometimes walk home for lunch with a parent. Fresh fruit, Spanish

Spain's Trains

The Red Nacional de Ferrocarriles (RENFE) train system spans 9,500 miles (15,200 kilometers) across Spain. The tracks are broad gauge and were installed for steam engines to have easier ascents in the mountain ranges. The broad gauge tracks differ from those that span most of Europe, and this issue isolated Spanish trains for years. Today some European trains are able to widen their wheel base in order to travel on Spain's tracks.

Passengers of the RENFE might pay around 9 euros (U.S.$11.99) for a tourist-class ticket from Barcelona to Figueres, a two-hour ride.

Spain also has a popular high-speed railroad. The first Alta Velocidad Espanola (AVE), opened in April 1992. It runs between Madrid and Seville. The new line reduced the usual train travel time between the two cities from six to two and a half hours. The train travels at speeds approaching 186 miles (298 km) per hour.

The AVE high-speed trains were also named for the Spanish word "ave," which means "bird."

Central Government's Expenditures on Education

In the past 20 years, government officials have gradually increased the amount of the gross domestic product (GDP) dedicated to education.

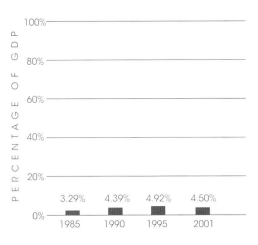

PERCENTAGE OF GDP

1985	1990	1995	2001
3.29%	4.39%	4.92%	4.50%

Source: U.N. Common Database

tortillas made with eggs, meat or fish, and some cheese is typical lunch fare. After lunch, they return to school for their afternoon classes. School-provided lunches are not common in Spanish schools, so many children bring lunches to eat.

Classes end around 4 P.M., but it depends on the length of the midday break. At the end of the day, most children walk home or attend an after-school activity such as *fútbol* (soccer), basketball, or chess.

Parents and community members often sponsor after-school activities because most public schools only have funding for academics. They form clubs for sports and other activities, and children attend these clubs after school. The more popular activities include fútbol, basketball, performing in plays, dancing, singing, and bicycling.

Traveling fútbol and basketball club teams will practice three or four times a week and travel throughout the country to play teams of the same age. The best players may join national clubs and will play against teams from other European countries.

fútbol
FOOT-bole

After their activities, children head home where chores await them. They might help unload the dishwasher or set the table for a late-afternoon snack. Then, it's time for homework and a quick bath or shower before going to the public square to hang out with friends and walk with their family. Dinner comes sometime after 9 P.M., and they might not be in bed until midnight or later.

After school and on breaks, teens can be seen playing street fútbol.

17

Teen Scenes

A 12-year-old girl from Valencia, a city in eastern Spain, lives in an apartment with her mother, father, and younger brother.

Each morning, her parents wake her up and she heads to the kitchen for a breakfast of cereal.

She attends a German school in the city, and her father takes her to school by car each day. The school offers many classes in German, but also offers courses in English and Valencian.

School gets out at 2 P.M., and she must return home by taking the metro on her own.

Once she arrives at home, she performs some chores, relaxes for awhile, and then does her homework. The amount of homework varies each day, but it usually takes her an hour and a half or two hours to complete.

On Tuesday and Thursday afternoons, she plays basketball at a community club.

Dinner is served around 9 P.M., and her favorite meal is pizza.

When she isn't in school, she enjoys reading, playing basketball, or listening to music.

Another teen, who lives in a small rural part of Spain, resides in a whitewashed house with his grandparents, parents, older sister, and younger brother. He wakes up at 5:15 A.M., so he can help his parents with the daily chores,

After chores, he boards a school bus and greets his friends for the first time that day. The bus winds its way through the countryside, eventually making its way to the schoolhouse, which is 10 miles (16 km) away.

At school, his teacher begins with an English lesson and ends the day with mathematics.

Once the school day is done, the boy meets his friends outside for a game of fútbol, and they play until the bus arrives to take them back home again.

By 5 P.M., he is back at home and is helping his father repair a truck. He can smell the aroma of dinner coming from the kitchen, where his mother and sister are preparing a special dish. But he still has chores to finish and homework to complete before dinner will be served.

City or rural life, public or private school, teens in Spain commonly help with family chores and still find time to enjoy activities with friends.

Many Spanish schools have courtyards where students can gather to talk or study.

The Ciclos

ciclos
SEE-close

primer ciclo
pree-MAYR SEE-cloh

segundo ciclo
say-GOON-doh SEE-cloh

tercer ciclo
TAYR-sayr SEE-cloh

Elementary school is divided into sections known as *ciclos, or* cycles. The *primer ciclo,* or first cycle, covers years one and two, for ages 6 and 7. *Segundo ciclo,* or the second cycle, covers years three and four, for ages 8 and 9. *Tercer ciclo,* or the final cycle, covers years five and six, for ages 10 and 11. If students do not pass an exam after their primer or segundo ciclo, they may have to repeat a year of study, though less than 3 percent of elementary school students fail.

Students are evaluated each year and tested at the end of each ciclo to see if they can move to the next level. If a student does not pass the standard test, he or she may have to repeat the previous year unless he or she can pass a second test the next fall. But the Education Act of 1990, or LOGSE, stated that a student would only need to repeat a year twice before he or she would be

About 91 percent of secondary students pass the additional standards test, which covers reading, math, science, and history.

educación secundaria obligatoria

eh-dyoo-KAY-siohn
say-cun-DAH-ryah
ob-lee-gah-TOH-ryah

passed to the next grade. At age 12, students begin *educación secundaria obligatoria (ESO)*, or secondary education, which consists of two two-year ciclos. Students take a mix of classes that are required or optional. The required subjects include natural and social sciences, history, geography, physical education, art, Spanish, literature, mathematics, Catholic religion (or history of religions, ethics, or study hour for non-Catholic students), music, technology, and a foreign language. In the last year of their primer ciclo, students must choose two extra classes from natural science, art, music, or technology. Elective courses—such as additional languages—are available for students in their segundo cycle of studies.

Eugenia Perea, a student from a small town in Cataluna, focuses on languages in her elective courses. She takes Spanish, English, Greek, Latin, and Catalan—a regional language. "I like the humanities," she said. "I want to be a translator and an interpreter."

Students who complete their secondary education are awarded a "graduate of secondary education" certificate,

In the final years of study, English is a manditory class.

which enables them to enter higher education or receive specialized vocational training. This certificate is a basic requirement for most jobs in Spain. Those students who do not complete secondary school are given a school certificate, and may prepare for specific careers that do not require a four-year college degree, such as an office assistant or a barber. More than 60 percent of students continue their education until they are 18 years old.

Getting Into College

For high school students, the college entrance process begins at the age of 16, when they must decide if they want to go to college or get a technical education for a specific job. Those who choose college will spend the next two years preparing, with such courses as natural sciences, mathematics, languages, and humanities. During the second year of college preparation, students are able to choose some courses on their own.

Finally, at the end of the second year of college preparation, students take an exam known as the *Prueba General de Bachillerato*. Passing this exam allows students to attend colleges throughout the world. If they fail, they receive a certificate and can either choose to repeat the exam, attend vocational training, or drop out.

Graduation Ceremonies

In 2004, 61.8 percent of students finished their secondary school educations. The size and formality of graduation ceremonies depend on the size of the school and the city. In rural areas,

Around 90 percent of university students choose to attend a public university. Most college students attend the university closest to their home, where they will continue to live while attending classes.

most high school graduation ceremonies are small, casual affairs where students are joined by their families to mark the completion of their coursework. Graduates wear either their school uniforms or street clothes to walk up and receive their diplomas from their teachers or principals.

University

Spain has 75 universities, and 56 of those schools are run by the state. The rest are privately funded, some by the Catholic Church.

There are two types of universities for graduates of secondary school. University schools offer three-year courses in vocational and nonacademic fields. University colleges offer three-year courses focusing on academics only. Graduates of university colleges earn a *licencia en estudios académicos,* or license in academic studies, while graduates from university schools earn a diploma. In 2004, about 62 percent of males and about 76 percent of females enrolled in a university completed their studies by graduating.

licencia en estudios académicos
lee-SEN-see-yah en ess-TOO-dee-yos ack-ah-DEM-ee-cohs

23

More than a third of Spain's citizens live in the 50 largest Spanish cities, such as Madrid, Barcelona, Valencia, and Seville.

2

Sharing Space

THERE ARE MANY KINDS OF HOMES THROUGHOUT SPAIN—from small wooden dwellings in remote villages to large villas just outside the cities. Older towns often have traditional buildings facing a courtyard with benches, flowers, and perhaps a fountain or a place for young children to play.

But Spain's larger cities are almost entirely made up of apartment buildings. Most people live in two-bedroom apartments that are rented or owned as condominiums. Single-family homes are rare. Many of the buildings are whitewashed and feature sloping clay roofs that protect against the intense heat from

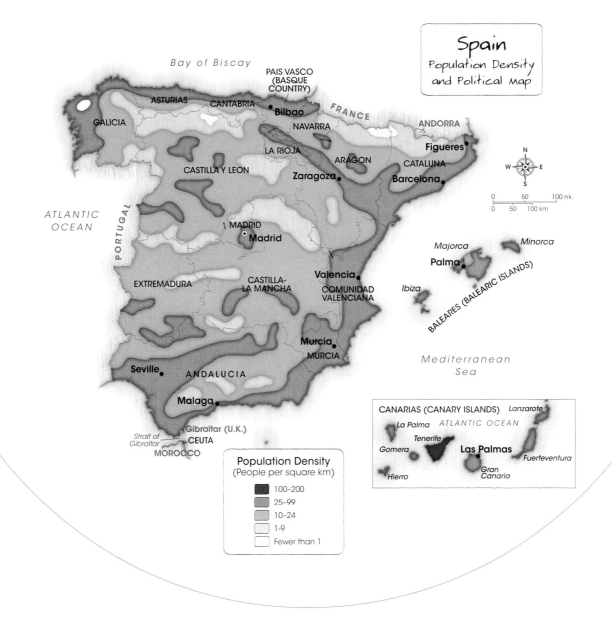

Spain
Population Density and Political Map

Bay of Biscay

ASTURIAS · CANTABRIA
PAIS VASCO (BASQUE COUNTRY)
FRANCE

GALICIA

● Bilbao

NAVARRA

ANDORRA

LA RIOJA

Figueres

CASTILLA Y LEON

ARAGON

CATALUNA

● Zaragoza

Barcelona ●

ATLANTIC OCEAN

PORTUGAL

↓ MADRID
⊛ **Madrid**

Majorca   Minorca

Palma ●

EXTREMADURA

CASTILLA-LA MANCHA

Valencia ●
COMUNIDAD VALENCIANA

Ibiza

BALEARES (BALEARIC ISLANDS)

N
W ✦ E
S

0   50   100 mi.
0 50 100 km

Murcia ●
MURCIA

Mediterranean Sea

Seville ●
ANDALUCIA

Malaga ●

Strait of Gibraltar
● Gibraltar (U.K.)
CEUTA
MOROCCO

Population Density
(People per square km)

- ■ 100–200
- ■ 25–99
- ■ 10–24
- □ 1-9
- □ Fewer than 1

CANARIAS (CANARY ISLANDS)   Lanzarote
La Palma   ATLANTIC OCEAN
Tenerife
Gomera   **Las Palmas** ●   Fuerteventura
Hierro   Gran Canaria

the bright sun. Summer temperatures can easily top 100 degrees Fahrenheit (37.8 degrees Celsius).

Though Spaniards are having smaller families than they used to, it is not uncommon for siblings to share bedrooms. Space is limited, especially in the larger cities, where most people live in apartments.

Urban teens typically live in apartments.

Rural Life

For most of Spain's history, country life was common for the population. But in the 1960s, that quickly began to change. People began to leave their farms and move to the city.

Since the mid-1900s, not much has changed for Spaniards living in the country. There families live in farm-houses constructed of clay and stone and painted white to guard against the hot sun. These homes can sometimes contain three or four bedrooms for larger families of six, seven, or more children who help tend to crops such as olive trees or feed sheep or cattle.

Traditionally, parents are expected to provide a home for their sons when

Today one third of Spain's population lives in the country.

they marry. That means many parents in rural areas expand upon their small homes to provide a place for their son's family to live.

Farmers grow olive trees for olive oil, or grape vines for wine. In some of the smallest and oldest villages, residents might be living without electricity or running water.

Menu of the Day

In Spain, breakfast is a brief, small meal—sometimes just juice and a roll. For a special treat, teenagers sometimes enjoy a hot chocolate beverage and *churros*, or deep-fried dough covered in sugar.

Lunch is considered the main meal of the day and often includes three courses. The first course is generally soup, salad, smoked salmon or cured meat, and vegetables such as tomatoes, carrots, corn, and potatoes. The main course is fresh fish, shrimp, or pork. Dessert is typically fresh fruit—such as mandarins or grapes—but may also include yogurt, ice cream, or flan (custard).

churros
CHEW-rohs

Spain
Topographical
Map

Bay of Biscay

Costa Verde

Cantabrian Mountains

Ebro River

FRANCE

P y r e n e e s

ANDORRA

Duero River

Costa Brava

Meseta Central

ATLANTIC OCEAN

PORTUGAL

★ Madrid

Costa Dorada

Costa del Azahar

Minorca

Tagus River

Majorca

Guadiana River

Ibiza

Balearic Islands

S i e r r a   M o r e n a

Guadalquivir River

Costa Blanca

Andalusian Plain

Mediterranean Sea

Costa de la Luz

Sierra Nevada

Costa del Sol

Strait of Gibraltar

MOROCCO

MOROCCO

Major train routes

N
W · E
S

0   50   100 mi.
0   50   100 km

Canary Islands

ATLANTIC OCEAN

Lanzarote

La Palma

Tenerife

Gomera

Fuerteventura

Hierro

Gran Canaria

In restaurants, it is rare for lunch to be served before 2 P.M. The busiest hours are from 2 P.M. to 4 P.M.

Another common dessert is *arroz con leche*, or rice with milk and cinnamon.

Spanish law requires most restaurants to provide a *menu del día*—three courses offered together for a discounted price—at lunch.

For many citizens, the few hours after lunch are still reserved for a *siesta*, a nap or rest time. While it's a less-common practice in recent years, most people take their naps at home if they can. Some shopkeepers even close up for a while. The pace of everything—even the traffic—slows down until the late afternoon.

arroz con leche
ah-ROSE cone LAY-chay

menu del día
MEN-you del DEE-ah

siesta
see-EHS-tah

A Typical Daily Menu

tapas
TOP-us

Breakfast	Lunch	Dinner
A roll and coffee, juice, or milk with cacao, or cocoa.	Paella or a three-course meal. The first course usually contains vegetables such as corn, potatoes, and squash. The second course contains smoked meat or fish—tuna, salmon, salt cod, or swordfish. The third course might contain a slice of fresh fruit—oranges, pears, cherries, or pomegranates—for dessert and sangria to drink.	Sometimes another three-course meal, but more often it's *tapas,* a smaller portion of meats and seafood, or a sandwich with wine and coffee. The word *tapas* means "no top." They began with the Spanish tradition of placing a slice of meat on top of a glass of wine.

It is common for a tapas bar to serve a variety of tapas, some with ham and tomatoes.

Fast Food a Favorite

International burger and sandwich chains such as McDonald's, Burger King, KFC, and Subway are also favorites among Spanish teens. While they like their food fast, they usually do not eat on the run. Most will take time to enjoy their meal at the restaurant or take it home to eat it.

A restaurant called VIPS is one of Spain's most popular fast-food chains. It sells national dishes from Spain, Mexico, and Italy. Spain's largest retail company owns the restaurants. In many VIPS restaurants, there is a shop with books, magazines, DVDs, CDs, and sports clothing.

Dinner usually does not start until after 9 P.M. Eating out is a real family occasion. Babies sit on their mothers' laps, and grandparents gather around to enjoy a meal together. It is also typical for women to cluster at one end of the table and men at the other. Good table manners are very important. For example, it is considered rude to keep hands hidden under the table. It is also important to consider the correct use of cutlery, in which the left hand holds the fork and the right hand holds the spoon or knife.

The Evening *Paseo*

Around 7 P.M. each evening, the streets and central squares of Spain's cities and towns

paseo
pah-SAY-oh

Flan is often served with a caramel topping.

suddenly swell with people. Young women, freshly showered and smartly dressed, chat and laugh with their friends. Teenagers take the evening paseo, or stroll, to try to impress or flirt with one another, but almost always from a distance.

As the youngsters spill out onto the streets, they are followed by grandparents and parents strolling hand-in-hand. It is an opportunity to cool down after a hot day and work up an appetite for the meal that awaits them later that evening.

Before dinner, couples often enjoy an evening paseo together.

Tasty Treats & Favorite Dishes

Spaniards love food, and they love to share it, usually savoring mealtime with large groups of friends and family.

One of the most popular dishes is *paella*. It is a mixture of rice, chicken, seafood such as shrimp and mussels, and flavorful herbs and spices like saffron. Some recipes call for chickpeas, sausages, or other meats like rabbit. Paella is typically a midday dish, but it is sometimes served at dinnertime.

paella
pah-AY-uh

Paella is considered Spain's national dish.

Gazpacho is a popular cold soup that the Spanish eat for lunch or dinner.

Another favorite traditional Spanish dish is *cocido,* a meat stew. There are three basic ingredients: meats, legumes (or beans), and vegetables such as corn, carrots, and potatoes. The stew is divided into three courses or servings. First, the broth is served, then the vegetables and finally the meats, which are sometimes shredded and mixed to fill *pringa,* or toasted bread rolls.

During summer months, a popular main dish is *gazpacho.* This cold soup is usually made with tomato, garlic, oil, pepper, and onion, and is served with bread.

Garlic, tomatoes, and olives, which are all grown in Spain,

cocido
coh-SEE-doh

pringa
PREEN-gah

gazpacho
gahs-PAH-cho

at the markets. Shoppers also will find vegetables such as artichokes, asparagus, carrots, and tomatoes.

Coastal regions are known for seafood, and teenagers living in the country's north-central Basque region enjoy perhaps the country's best seafood cuisine. There, fresh fish is sometimes combined with a delicious cream sauce, possibly inspired by France, which is just to the north. Common seafood served in Spain includes shrimp, mussels, lobster, crab, tuna, and swordfish.

Bedtimes, Curfews, & Punishments

Since dinnertime comes late, bedtime is also late for teens. In fact, even the youngest children in Spain stay up until 9 P.M. or 10 P.M. during the school year and teens may stay up as late as 11 P.M. or midnight. On the weekends, they may just be leaving the house at that time. A teen girl tells about a typical weekend with her friends: "We meet up around 11:30 or midnight and go out to the discos until about 3 [A.M.]"

Most teens are allowed to stay out, talking to friends, skateboarding, or riding bikes around the fountain in the town square long into the night. However, teens who break the rules or stay out too late are likely to get a stern lecture from their elders. Some of them may be grounded or lose privileges such as watching television or playing video games.

are ingredients in many Spanish dishes. Spain is the largest olive grower in the world, so it is no surprise that olive oil and olives themselves are common ingredients in the food. And Spain's warm climate and fertile soil mean most of the fruits and vegetables come fresh from nearby farms and are sold in the outdoor markets common in city streets. Oranges, mandarins, strawberries, avocados, and grapes are familiar sights

With more than 40 million residents, Spain has one of the largest populations in Europe.

3

Time Together

JUST LIKE PARENTS AROUND THE WORLD, SPANISH PARENTS LOVE THEIR CHILDREN, and sometimes they spoil them. Parents often spend more money on their children's clothing than on their own.

Children are almost always included in parties, too. It's not uncommon to see children sitting beside their parents late at night out for dinner or at a wedding or other celebration.

Babies and small children are welcome at restaurants no matter the time of day. Waiters and waitresses have even been known to take the tots around the restaurant, showing them off to fellow employees and other customers.

Parks and playgrounds are common throughout Spain, even in the tiniest villages where there is usually at least a swing set and sandbox.

Spain has one of the lowest birth rates in the world, and small families are the norm.

Big Family Then—Smaller Family Now

Until the past few decades, large families with as many as eight children were not uncommon in Spain. But recently Spaniards have been careful in planning the number of children they have, and have reduced the number of children being born per family.

In the 1950s and 1960s, farming became less common in Spain, and people migrated from rural areas into the cities. As families moved from the farms to the cities, there was less

Ethnic Groups

Spain has one of the more diverse populations in Europe. Although it was united in the 15th century and remains more than 90 percent Roman Catholic, Spain has kept many of its individual cultures and languages.

There are many regional cultures, including Andalusians, Basques, Castilians, Catalans, Galicians, and the Leonese. Each region is dedicated to its history, and many of the residents would prefer to identify themselves by that region rather than as Spanish.

Sabin Bizkarrelogorra Bravo lives in Bilbao in the Basque region. The teen boy considers himself Basque only—not Spanish. He explains:

"My point of view would be always from the view point of a Basque patriot, which would be the one that about 60 [percent] of Basque citizens have. It is only a minority that also feel Spanish."

Schoolchildren in each region learn both the national Spanish language—Castilian—and their own locally spoken language.

There are also several smaller groups, including Gitanos, Sephardic Jews and those known for farming and herding like the Agotes, Pasiegos, and Vaqueiros de Alzada. Gypsies, or the "Rom," as they sometimes call themselves, live throughout Spain. There are two main groups of gypsies—the Gitanos, who live primarily in the southern and central regions of Spain, and the Rumanos, who travel throughout the country.

Families might share a typical two-bedroom apartment near Plaza Mayor in Madrid.

need for large families to help tend to the crops and animals, so smaller families became more common. In addition, there was also not always enough housing for people in the cities. It became even more necessary for family members to share their homes and apartments with grandparents, aunts, uncles, and cousins. Extended families are still very common in Spain, where several generations sometimes live together.

Most teens are very close to their grandparents. That is because the Spanish care for the elderly as much as they do children.

Rarely are aging parents left alone in nursing homes or hospitals. Instead, they move into their children's homes to live with their grandchildren the rest of their days. Some grandparents might also care for their grandchildren while the parents work.

And since tradition holds that children do not move out of their parents' house until they are married, it is not unusual for people in their mid- and late-20s to still live with their parents.

Families often enjoyed at least two meals together each day. But, as with many other modern families, schedules have grown busier. Now teenagers are more likely to spend some of that mealtime away from home with their friends.

Gran Vía is one of the popular shopping areas in Madrid. The street is also known for its buildings, which are stunning examples of early 20th-century architecture.

Teens in Andalusia, in the southern Costa del Sol region of Spain, stroll the promenade.

Hanging Out With Friends

Spanish youths love to go out with their friends. They go shopping, play sports, or chat in the streets.

Until they are well into their teenage years, boys tend to play with boys and girls with girls. But the two groups often mingle during the evening paseo, or at parties.

Dating often does not start until a teen is 13 years old, but it is usually more common for those 14 and older as they begin high school. Even then, dating is most often a group activity with teens hanging out in the town square or at the local arcade playing video games.

Friends meet in parks, playgrounds, or the town's central square to play games such as basketball and fútbol. Often, they will play until curfew.

What to Wear?

Spanish teens are among the most fashionable in all of Europe, and shopping for clothes is a popular pastime. In the past few decades, Spain's fashion industry has become a major force around the world, and the largest cities are some of the most fashionable. Madrid and Barcelona hold their own fashion weeks.

However, that also means that clothes are expensive, and bargain clothing stores are rare. Families who cannot afford the latest fashions shop in street markets for their clothes. While name brands are important to young people, the quality of the clothes is just as important. And Spanish clothes from the markets tend to be high in quality and low in price. The clothing company Zara is Spain's most popular brand, offering clothes for men, women, and children. H&M and Benetton are also favorites.

Teenage girls usually wear pants instead of skirts. Jeans, T-shirts, and athletic shoes are common clothes for both boys and girls.

Fashion Week in Madrid

The organizers of Madrid's fashion week recently set a new rule when it comes to the models they choose. Models with a body mass index of less than 18 will not be allowed to walk on the runway. This new rule regarding models who are too thin is the first ever of its kind.

"Fashion is a mirror, and many teenagers imitate what they see on the catwalk," said one of Madrid's officials.

For teenage girls who look to the models as the standard for a woman's weight, Madrid's decision is an important one.

During the Epiphany parade in central Seville, a girl throws candy from a float.

4 Fiestas of Faith & Tradition

MORE THAN 90 PERCENT OF SPAIN'S RESIDENTS CLAIM CATHOLICISM as their religion. The church and its priests play a major role in the daily lives of most of Spain's citizens. Every village has at least one church, and the priest is often treated as a family member. Most Spaniards are baptized in the church, married in the church as adults, and buried by the church when they die. Because of the emphasis on their faith, most of the holidays celebrated by the Spanish are related to the Catholic religion. But some Spanish celebrations are related to something completely different—the art of bullfighting.

47

National Holidays & Festivals

Imagine running through narrow, cobblestone streets being chased by a herd of charging bulls. Then imagine doing it on purpose. That's what happens every July in Pamplona and cities throughout Spain the entire year. It's called *el encierro,* the annual "running of the bulls."

el encierro

el ehn-see-AIR-oh

During the weeklong Sanfermines festival in Pamplona, a pack of six bulls and steers runs through the center of town to the bullring every day.

Since then, the running of the bulls has become one of Spain's most famous events. Large numbers of young men—and some women—wear white shirts, white pants, and red neck scarves as they sprint down the streets and jump out of the way as the pack of bulls races past. Some try to touch the bulls because it is thought to bring good luck. Dozens of people are often severely injured each year, either trampled or gored with the bulls' horns. Some even die. Yet the tradition continues, attracting runners from around the world, eager to prove they are brave enough to run with the bulls.

Cities in Spain often have festivals celebrating their unique heritage or history. But Carnival is a major event celebrated throughout the country before the start of the Christian observance of Lent, the 40 days before Easter. There are large parades and parties where people wear brightly colored costumes and masks or dress as animals.

Many of the parades feature *gigantes*, or giants, and *cabezudos*, or big-headed characters. The giants represent Spanish kings and queens. The cabezudos —some of which can look quite scary—represent groups of outsiders that have tried to take over Spain throughout the country's history.

The bulls charge through the streets on their way to the bullfighting ring. The festival began in the mid-1800s when runners started joining the bulls as they ran from the edge of town to the bullfighting ring.

gigantes
hee-GAHN-tays

cabezudos
kah-bay-SOO-dohs

49

Cabezudos are worn in the procession of the Gigantes y Cabezudos during the Fiesta de san Fermin in Pamplona.

Spanish Celebrations

Every one of Spain's cities, towns, and villages has its own fiesta, or festival. In small villages, these parties may last just a day or two. In the biggest cities, they can stretch on for a week or longer. People traditionally return to the town where they grew up to attend the fiesta.

Most fiestas include a quiet religious ceremony along with non-religious events celebrating favorite local food, music, sports, clothing, and dance. The theme of the fiesta usually focuses on a popular local person or character.

One such fiesta takes place every May 15 in Madrid. People celebrate San Isidro, the patron saint of farmers. People walk to a meadow to drink holy water from a fountain and they eat and drink for several days. Men and women wear traditional outfits. Men wear white neckerchiefs, black-and-white check jackets, waistcoats, and caps. Women wear frilly dresses and head scarves.

At some festivals there is a raffle

with a lamb or a calf as a prize. The money collected is used to throw a party for the village's single young men and women in hopes they might meet a future husband or wife.

Religious Holidays

Día de Pascua, or Easter, is Spain's most important religious holiday, marking the resurrection of Jesus Christ.

However, the celebrations during Holy Week—from Palm Sunday to Easter Sunday—are the most spectacular. Marchers take to the streets wearing hooded robes, and hundreds of men carry special statues of Jesus and the Virgin Mary while dressed in jeweled and embroidered outfits. Vibrant songs and dances greet the parade as it moves down the street.

During Holy Week In Burgos, in northern Spain, Christians carry a statue of Christ through the streets of the city.

Navidad, or Christmas, is a Christian religious holiday that honors the birth of Christ. It has only recently become popular in Spain, and it has fast become a favorite holiday among children and teens. Papá Noel visits boys and girls, showering them with presents on Navidad.

Año Nuevo, or New Year's Day, is another favorite holiday. The evening before Año Nuevo ends with people eating 12 grapes or raisins apiece. Gulping them down one at a time as the clock strikes each toll is said to bring good luck for the coming year.

Día de Reyes, or Day of the Kings, caps the Navidad and Año Nuevo holidays. On January 6, three men play the roles of the three kings who were said to have first visited Jesus Christ in the manger, and they pass out gifts to children. However, some Spanish families are

In Madrid, people construct a large Navidad display of lights.

In Bilbao, women pass out roscón de reyes on Día de Reyes.

switching to Papá Noel leaving gifts on the morning of Navidad. On January 6, families traditionally eat chocolate and *roscón de reyes*, a traditional fruit cake. Inside the cake, the baker hides prizes, usually tiny statues of the three kings.

roscón de reyes

rah-SCONE de RAY-ehs

Religious Coming of Age

Another common celebration for youngsters is Primera Comunion, or First Communion. This religious ceremony marks a young person's first participation in the sacrament of the Holy Eucharist in the Catholic Church. It is a major event in Spanish families and usually takes place when a child is 7 or 8 years old, and reaches what Catholics call the "age of reason."

Children dressed in traditional white clothing celebrate their First Communion in Seville.

Celebrations marking the occasion can number more than 100 people, over-taking a restaurant with well-wishers bearing gifts. Pressed suits for boys and white dresses for girls are typical attire for Primera Comunion.

Confirmation, which takes place between the ages of 16 and 17, is another important time for many teens. During this ceremony, teens confirm their faith in the Catholic Church.

Another sacrament in the Catholic

Church is marriage. Weddings are large events in Spain, with at least 200 guests, including the entire extended family and many friends.

Men are offered cigars and women often receive small gifts. During the ceremony, the groom's mother walks her son down the aisle to "give him away."

The bride's father is expected to keep the bride hidden until the ceremony begins, and he then escorts her to the ceremony, which usually takes place in church at midday. Afterward, there is a meal and reception at a hotel, restaurant,

The Plaza España is a popular spot for couples in Seville to take wedding photos.

Calendar of Public & Religious Holidays

Año Nuevo (New Year's Day)—January 1	Santiago (St. James' Day)—July 25
Día de Reyes (Day of the Kings)—January 6	Asuncion (Assumption)—August 15
Carnival (before the start of Lent)—40 days before Easter	Día de la Hispanidad (Hispanic Day)—October 12
Jueves Santo (Holy Thursday)—the Thursday before Easter	Todos los Santos ((All Saints' Day)—November 1
Viernes Santo (Good Friday)—the Friday before Easter	Día de la Constitucion (Constitution Day)—December 6
Día de Pascua (Easter Sunday)	Immaculada Concepcion (Immaculate Conception)—December 8
Día del Trabajo (Labor Day)—May 1	Navidad (Christmas)—December 25
Corpus Christi—May or June	
Sanfermines (includes running of the bulls)—July 6-14	

or hall. The celebration can go well into the early morning of the next day.

Funerals

Funerals follow a person's death almost immediately unless the person dies on a Sunday or a holiday. Before burial or cremation—the burning of the body into ashes—family members stand watch over the coffin all night as friends and relatives pay their respects. Though there may be some loud crying or wailing, most Spanish funerals are somber events.

Most of the dead are not buried right away. Instead, they are placed in above-ground structures. They stay there for five years before being buried in a common grave with other coffins. Todos los Santos, or All Saints' Day, calls for families to visit the graves of deceased loved ones. But it is far from a sad ceremony. Families bring food and drink to the cemeteries to remember and honor the dead while celebrating time together with the living.

A Spanish cemetery often features above-ground enclosures.

The service industry makes up about 64 percent of all jobs in Spain.

5

Earning Cash

THE SPANISH ECONOMY HAS MADE GAINS IN THE past few decades, especially since becoming a part of the European Union in 1986. In 2006, the country's unemployment rate fell to 8.15 percent, the lowest since 1979. Spain's strong family tradition makes the unemployment rate easier to handle. Families support each other, and those with jobs help those without—even throughout large, extended families.

The service sector makes up Spain's largest portion of the economy. Service jobs include those careers where workers provide a service to

Bay of Biscay

FRANCE

ANDORRA

Spain
Land Use Map

ATLANTIC
OCEAN

PORTUGAL

Madrid

Minorca

Majorca

Ibiza

Balearic Islands

Mediterranean
Sea

Strait of
Gibraltar

MOROCCO

Canary Islands
La Palma   ATLANTIC OCEAN   Lanzarote
Gomera   Tenerife
Hierro   Gran
Canaria   Fuerteventura

N
W   E
S

0   50   100 mi.
0   50   100 km

Land Use
- Cropland
- Goats and sheep
- Forests
- Fruit and olives
- Manufacturing
- Nonagricultural land

the public. For example, people who work in restaurants, in hotels, as housekeepers, or as gardeners would all be part of the service industry. Tourism provides the most jobs within the service industry, and teens often find employment opportunities.

Working the Way Up

Most young people are too busy with school or other activities to work too many hours at a part-time job. Still, the most common jobs for teens are as waiters, waitresses, and dishwashers in restaurants. Spanish law requires people to be the age of 16 before they begin working, and if they are younger than 18, their parents' permission is required. Most starting jobs pay around 3 euros (U.S.$3.99) per hour. This amount is roughly Spain's minimum wage—considerably lower than the European average of 5.65 euros (U.S.$7.52) per hour. Other teens help coach a basketball or fútbol team. On occasion, youths can pick up odd jobs helping a neighbor with chores or childcare, but the Spanish usually rely on their own families for that kind of work.

The service industry offers job opportunities to teens.

Moms at Work

For many years, women in Spain were expected to stay home, raise the children, cook, and clean. But that has changed dramatically in the past 20 years. Now women make up about 36 percent of the workforce and some work high-profile jobs as mayors, ambassadors, judges, and leaders in government and universities. However, discrimination still exists. Spanish women ages 30 to 44 earn about 79 percent of what men who have similar qualifications for the same jobs make.

Labor Force by Occupation

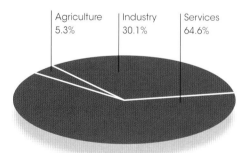

| Agriculture 5.3% | Industry 30.1% | Services 64.6% |

Source: United States Central Intelligence Agency. *The World Factbook—Spain.*

61

A teen might work as a railway host, assisting passengers during their journey on the AVE high speed train in Madrid.

Young people are also joining the workforce much later than their parents did. They are staying in school longer, and many are perfecting their English skills so they can work in international business.

In their final years of high school, students who will not attend college receive "FP" training or "professional formation" courses. The students in these classes train for a specific kind of job—such as a clerk or a laborer— that they may pursue after graduation.

Out on Their Own

Teens who work while they are in school are likely to work at any job they can find. Usually they will work in the summers to help earn some spending money, and sometimes they will work part time during the school year to help earn money for their family's needs.

Most will not get their first serious job until they turn 18 years old. Because unemployment is high in Spain, young people are happy just to get a job after graduation. Once a teen graduates, his or her first job may depend largely on whom he or she is related to. Family members often give hiring preference to their own relatives.

Depending on the path they chose in high school, teens can get jobs ranging from being a clerk in a government office, a construction worker, or a waiter. If they pursued a higher, more formal education, they might find a job at a bank or in the lower level of a large corporation.

The minimum wage in Spain is 540.9 euros (U.S.$720.48) per month.

Jai alai players wear a cesta-punta, or wicker glove.

6

Game On

CHECKERS, CHESS, AND CARD GAMES ARE VERY POPULAR IN SPAIN, with outdoor tables in plazas and cafés reserved for competition. Monopoly and Parchesi are popular board games with teens as well.

One favorite street game common in the main plaza at night is jai alai. The fast-paced game is usually played with a ball made of goat skin. The object is to take turns using a special wicker glove to hit a ball against the wall.

If you get it past your opponent, you can score points.

Video games played on Sony Play Stations or Nintendo units have also become very popular, and the playing of these games has led to fewer youths playing outdoors.

In parks or on vacation, teens often gather to have elaborate scavenger hunts. They roam large areas searching for clues or objects. The group that collects the most objects wins.

cesta-punta
SEHS-tah-POON-tah

65

Stamp collecting is popular among Spanish youth. Teens often inherit collections from their fathers or mothers. These stamps depict their favorite soccer or basketball stars. They also like to collect clothing and posters from their favorite soccer club. Others collect pins with favorite celebrities or sayings on them and key rings.

Hanging Out & Having Fun

Teens get together to do nothing much at all. On weekends, teenagers are often found at the beach, shopping, and hanging out. Sometimes they go to movies or chat in cafés. They also enjoy skateboarding and inline skating in many of Spain's large central plazas.

Spanish teens are big fans of cell

National Parks Under Increasing Pressure

More than 9 percent of Spain's total land area is designated as protected land. There are more than 570 protected areas in the country. Spain was the first European country to establish a formal national parks system. The country's vast open fields, pristine forests, and mountainous regions have helped preserve habitats for a variety of birds, mammals, and other wildlife. The areas are popular tourist destinations for hikers, campers, and bird watchers.

However, those areas are coming under increasing pressure from people who want to use the land to build homes, hotels, and offices. Years of drought have also put parts of Spain in danger of becoming a desert.

phones. They call each other to make plans, share gossip, send text messages, or take pictures of each other.

Spanish youths have perfected short message service (SMS), a special language for text-messaging on their cell phones. Words are shortened to limit the number of buttons pressed, but the message remains clear.

Internet is another way for teens to keep in touch. Students in Spain get most of their Internet access at school, but an

Skateboarders perform tricks on the plaza of the Museu d'Art Contemporani de Barcelona.

There are more than 38 million cell phones in use throughout Spain.

increasing number of families are logging on and surfing the Web. In 2005, more than 17 million Spaniards had access to the Internet at home, work, or school. That's almost half of the country.

Most Internet access is through a dial-up telephone connection, but more companies are providing broadband or high-speed Internet connections for a monthly fee.

Students in Spain use the Internet for their homework, but they are just as likely to use it for fun. They e-mail friends, visit chat rooms, send instant messages, or look up the latest news about their favorite band or movie star.

Reading is a hobby among some Spanish young people. About 98 percent of all Spaniards above the age of 15 are literate, one of the highest percentages in the world. Popular books are adventure novels, comic books, detective fiction, and science fiction. Many of the books are sold at kiosks, or small street-side stands.

Favorite titles are Spanish translations of many English-language authors, including Stephen King, John Steinbeck, J.R.R. Tolkein, and Jane Austen.

One of the most popular forms for young people is the *fotonovela*, or photo novel. These books feature pictures of people posed in situations with word "bubbles" coming out of

fotonovela
foh-toh-no-vel-lah

their mouths, similar to cartoons or comic books.

Dances & Discos

Older teens in Spain frequent discos and bars on weekends. Discos feature dance floors, bright lights, and loud music.

Some younger teens are also allowed into clubs in Spain. In 2002, the drinking age was raised from 16 years old to 18 years old because of a rise in the number of alcohol-related accidents

A dance floor in Ibiza is crowded with teens and young adults.

Flamenco

The tradition of flamenco is uniquely Spanish, and southern Spain is credited with creating the colorful blend of music and dance.

Most flamenco exists in three distinct parts—the song, the dance, and the guitar. The music and dancing are usually very dramatic, and both are joined by soaring singing.

involving young people. Still, the age requirement is rarely enforced. Because drinking at family celebrations and other festivals is so common in Spain, bartenders rarely worry about the age of their customers.

There are also a number of regular "rave" parties held at homes or rented halls where older teens stay late dancing to loud music.

Music is Always Popular

From flamenco to jazz to rock, music is a major part of the Spanish culture.

Spanish teens love rock and pop music, and many of their favorite artists are performers from the United States and England. Performers such as Alicia Keys, Beyonce, Christina Aguilera, Jay-Z, and Usher are a few of the international musicians that Spanish teens listen to.

Spanish performers are also popular, and include artists such as Tony Santos, David Bisbal, Ricky Martin, Natalia, Paulina Rubio, and the band La Oreja De Van Gogh.

Some teens favor "root-rock," a form of music that takes traditional flamenco singing and adds a more upbeat rhythm. Others like rave music, which uses heavy beats and electronics.

Rap and hip-hop are also growing in popularity, sometimes imported from other Spanish-speaking countries in South America.

Sports Role Models

While Spanish teens are just as likely to choose their parents as role models as anybody famous, popular culture plays an important role.

Raul Gonzalez Blanco

By scoring a goal every two matches, Blanco seems on track to beat the existing all-time goal scoring record set for his soccer team, Real Madrid. After being named top scorer in Spain in 1999 and 2001, he also helped his team win three Champions League titles, two Intercontinental Cups, and four Spanish championships.

Beatriz Ferrer-Salat

In 2004, Ferrer-Salat won the individual bronze in dressage in her third Olympic Games. She also led the Spanish team to its first silver medal in dressage.

Severiano Ballesteros

Going pro at the age of 16, "Seve" has won more than 70 professional golf tournaments, including winning the Masters twice and the British Open three times. He has been called the most successful player in the history of Spanish golf. He was inducted into the World Golf Hall of Fame in 1997.

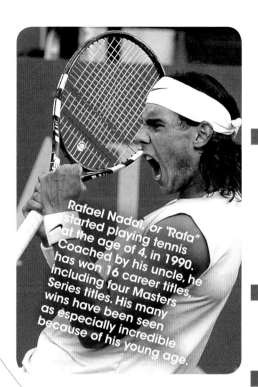

Rafael Nadal, or "Rafa" started playing tennis at the age of 4, in 1990. Coached by his uncle, he has won 16 career titles, including four Masters Series titles. His many wins have been seen as especially incredible because of his young age.

Turn up the Radio

Spain is a nation of radio listeners. In fact, they listen to the radio more than they watch television, with 16 million people listening at some point each day. There are about 35 million radios in Spain, and there are a number of popular local and national radio stations. Music is by far the most listened to radio format.

Movies & Movie Stars

While movies have lost some of their popularity as television choices have improved, a night out at the movies is still a favorite among teenagers. There are also a number of outdoor or drive-in theaters that are popular in the summer.

Teenagers love to go to some of the newer multiscreen theaters, which can have 15 different movies playing at once. Many of the films are some of the United States' most popular. They are dubbed with Spanish-speaking actors reading the lines or have Spanish subtitles at the bottom of the screen. Some of Spain's biggest movie stars are Antonio Banderas, Javier Bardem, and Penelope Cruz. Movies such as *Belle Epoque, Barcelona*, and *All About My Mother*, which won an Academy Award for best foreign language film in 1999, have been successful.

Other popular stars include Leonor Watling, from *Talk To Her*, Paz Vega from *Spanglish*, and Ernesto Alterio, from *Both Sides of the Bed*.

Going to movies is a popular pastime for Spanish teens.

Turn on the TV

In addition to movies, television provides entertainment to Spanish teens. While Spain did not get its first broadcast network until 1956, it has made up for lost time. Roughly 86 percent of Spanish households have at least one color television set.

Spanish television has one public station that is broadcast on two channels. It has a mix of shows, including news, drama, fiction, sports, sitcoms, and game shows.

The commercial stations have movies and a mix of programs much like the public stations. Game shows, reality shows, and Spanish soap operas are among the most popular programs

Director Pedro Almodovar

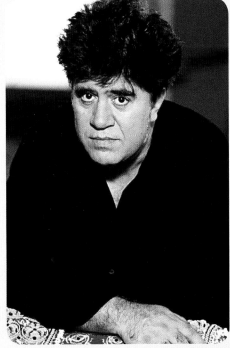

Spanish director Pedro Almodovar has introduced films featuring Antonio Banderas and Penelope Cruz, and his movies continue to draw huge audiences in Spain. Almodovar's movies have won or have been nominated for a number of awards, including Academy Awards in the United States.

His movies include: *Hable con Ella (Talk to Her)*, *Todo Sobre Mi Madre (All About My Mother)*, and *La Mala Educacion (Bad Education)*.

among Spanish TV viewers.

One of the most popular shows is called *Supervivientes*, a reality show on which contestants in remote places compete to survive the longest and to win large prizes. Another popular reality show is *Gran Hermano,* on which contestants live together in one place while being monitored 24 hours a day.

Favorite Activities

Spain's national activity is bullfighting, and some consider it an art. There are about 500 permanent bullfighting rings throughout Spain. Old and young people alike attend bullfights. And

Reality shows, like *Gran Hermano,* are becoming more popular in Spain.

there is no denying the spectacle. During an afternoon's *corrida,* or bull-fight, three matadors, or bullfighters, take on two bulls apiece. A matador is dressed in a tight costume adorned with

corrida
coh-REE-dah

fine threads and jewels and waves a blood-red flag to get the bull to charge. The crowd roars with approval as the bull makes a pass.

In the first stage of the corrida, the matador tests the bull with sweeps of his or her cape. The matador will carefully

The bullring in Málaga can hold up to 15,000 people. It also houses a bullfighting museum.

Matadors

Bullfighting began in the mid-16th century. It has become a national symbol of Spain and people from all over the world go to see the battle between matador and bull.

Popular matadors are treated like pop stars in Spain, mostly because of the mystery and danger associated with the art of fighting bulls. Between 24,000 and 40,000 bulls are killed each year, and at least 40 bullfighters have been killed by bulls in the ring since the sport began. One of the most famous bullfighters in history, Manolete, was killed by a bull in 1947.

A recent change to bullfighting is the presence of women in the sport. Cristina Sanchez made her first performance as a matador a week before her 21st birthday in 1993, and fought in Ecuador and Mexico. She is one of the best-known bullfighters in Spain and was one of the first prominent female matadors. But Sanchez retired in 1999, complaining that male prejudice prevented her from booking performances. She said:

"I've never traded on the fact that I am a woman; I've never used it to get ahead, but I've certainly suffered because of it ... When you lose the sense of joy in what you do it's best just to call it a day."

Another famous bullfighter is Julian Lopez, or "El Juli." Born in 1981, El Juli started his career at the age of 15 and was declared the number one bullfighter in 1999. He is most famous for his ability to face any bull, no matter how fierce.

A bull passes by the popular matador El Juli.

observe the bull for any weaknesses.

Next, two *picadors*, assistants on horseback, enter the ring. Their job is to stab the bull in the back of the neck. The result of this wound is a lowering of the bull's head for the rest of the fight.

In the next stage of the corrida, three more assistants will place *banderillas*, or pointed sticks, into the bull's neck. This act results in a further loss of blood for the bull, and it also encourages the bull to charge.

In the final section of the corrida, the matador attracts the bull with a large cape. The bull makes numerous

picadors
PEE-cah-doors

banderillas
ban-dah-REE-yahs

Spanish matador Jesuli de Torrecera performs a pass during a bullfight in the Maestranza bullring in Seville.

passes at the matador, whose skill is judged by how close he or she is able to get to the bull. In the final pass, the matador pierces the bull's heart with a sword. If the matador performs superbly, the audience will react by waving handkerchiefs. A matador who performs well will receive one ear of the bull. One who performs even better will receive both of the bull's ears. And a matador who performs with extraordinary skill

sometimes receives both ears and the tail of the bull.

While bullfighting is the activity most associated with Spain, fútbol, or soccer, is easily the most celebrated. Real Madrid is the country's most beloved team, attracting more than 130,000 fans to watch Saturday and Sunday evening matches in a huge stadium just outside Madrid. Other cities in Spain have their own teams, and

Real Madrid takes on another Spanish team, Celta de Vigo, at a soccer match in their home stadium.

From Seve to Sergio

Spain has given the golf world some of its most famous and successful players. First, there was Seve Ballesteros, who won the British Open in 1979, 1984 and 1988. He also won the Masters Tournament at Augusta, Georgia, in 1980 and 1983.

Today Spain's golf hero is Sergio Garcia, a young and energetic competitor and a regular challenger in many tournaments.

Spain has more than 200 golf courses, and the sport is gaining more players every year.

Sergio Garcia's nickname is El Niño. He has spent most of his career in the top 10 of the official world golf rankings.

when one of them wins, the entire city erupts in celebration. Fans swarm the streets, tooting horns, shooting fireworks, and waving flags for hours.

Not only is it the country's biggest spectator sport, but young people everywhere play fútbol as well. From the biggest cities to the smallest villages, youths are kicking balls across wide fields or passing them back and forth in the quiet corner of an alley.

While boys were once the

The Museo del Prado houses thousands of works of art, including pieces by the Spanish artists Diego Velázquez and Francisco Goya.

dominant fútbol players in Spain, a growing number of girls are also playing. There are special summer camps dedicated for boys and girls to learn new skills and strategies.

Because schools generally do not have many school-sponsored after-school activities or sports teams, students rely on outside groups and teams. Athletic events like fútbol and basketball are popular, as well as art, reading, and language clubs. Chapters of the Boy Scouts and Girl Scouts are also active throughout Spain.

World-Class Museums

Visiting museums is a popular pastime for all Spaniards, partly because of Spain's prominent museums, including the Prado in Madrid, and the Guggenheim in Bilbao.

Pablo Picasso is one of Spain's most celebrated artists, and there are two Picasso museums in Spain—one in Barcelona and one in Málaga—that feature his paintings and sculptures. Salvador Dali, another of Spain's most famous artists, has a museum dedicated to his work in Figueres, just outside of Barcelona. Dali's paintings often depict unusual images like melting clocks, twisted bodies, and haunted faces.

Looking Ahead

SPANISH TEENAGERS HAVE MUCH TO LOOK FORWARD TO.
Their communities are working hard to provide educational and recreational opportunities for them, and these efforts will be noticeable in the future generation of Spain's adults.

In a country where people love to take a siesta, teens are working hard to make sure their dreams for the future are attainable. More than ever, Spanish teens are choosing to attend universities and attain higher educations. With their educations, they will be able to help move their country forward.

While they are working hard, they also appreciate the traditions of the past. Like their parents and grandparents, they embrace many of Spain's oldest customs and celebrations, such as bullfighting and flamenco, while forging new traditions in areas such as fashion and music.

At a Glance

Official name: Kingdom of Spain

Capital: Madrid

People

Population: 40,397,842

Population by age group:
0 to 14 years: 14.4%
15 to 64 years: 67.8%
65 years and over: 17.7%

Life expectancy at birth: 79.65 years

Official language: Castilian Spanish

Other common languages: Catalan, Galician, Basque

Religion:
Roman Catholic: 94 %
Other: 6 %

Legal ages
Alcohol consumption: 18
Driver's license: 18
Employment: 16
Marriage: 16
Military service: 20
Voting: 18

Government

Type of government: Parliamentary monarchy

Chief of state: King

Head of government: President and prime minister

Lawmaking body: Las Cortes Generales (General Courts) consists of the Senado (Senate) and the Congreso de los Diputados (Congress of Deputies)

Administrative divisions: 17 autonomous communities and two autonomous cities

Independence: 1492, unification of several kingdoms

National symbols: Coat of arms represents the five kingdoms of Castilla, Leon, Aragón, Navarra, and Granada.

Geography

Total area: 201,913 square miles (504,782 square kilometers)

Climate: Temperate; sunny and hot in the summer in the interior; cooler and cloudier along the coast; cloudy and cold winters inland with somewhat sunnier and warmer winters along the coast

Highest point: Pico do Teide (Tenerife) on Canary Islands, 12,195 feet (3,718 meters)

Lowest point: Atlantic Ocean, sea level

Major rivers: Tagus, Río Ebro, Río Duero, Río Guadiana, Río Guadalquivir, Río Mino

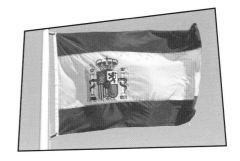

Major landforms: Pyrenees Mountains in the north; large plateau in the country's midsection

Economy

Currency: euro

Major natural resources: Coal, lignite, iron ore, copper, lead, zinc, uranium, tungsten, mercury, pyrites, magnesite, fluorspar, gypsum, sepiolite, kaolin, potash

Major agricultural products: Grain, vegetables, olives, wine grapes, sugar beets, citrus, beef, pork, poultry, dairy products, fish

Major exports: Cars, food ingredients, medicine, clothing, footwear

Major imports: Machinery and equipment, fuels, chemicals, food ingredients, consumer goods, measuring and medical control instruments

Historical Timeline

Christian victory at battle
of Navas de Tolosa is the
beginning of the end of
Moorish rule

Arab and Berber
forces from northern
Africa cross Strait of
Gibraltar to occupy
Iberian peninsula

 City-states begin to
appear in Greece

Inca civilization
flourishes in
South America

| 1100 B.C. | 800 B.C | A.D. 409 | 711 | 800 | c.1000 | 1013 | 1212 |

Internal strife splits
Moorish Spain
into small, feuding
kingdoms

Phoenician traders
establish colony at
Cádiz in southern
Iberia

Charlemagne
crowned emperor
of the Holy Roman
Empire

Visigoths take over
entire Iberian
peninsula

 Historical World Event

King Ferdinand and Queen isabella's army conquers Granada after a long fight, defeating the last of the Moors in Spain; Muslims and Jews are forced to convert to Catholicism or leave Spain; Christopher Columbus reaches the Americas

 James Watt patents the steam engine, initiating the Industrial Revolution

Spain loses control over Cuba and the Philippines in Spanish American War

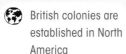 British colonies are established in North America

1347	1492	1540	1600's	1702-1714	1769	1808-1814	1898

Spanish explorer Francisco Vasquez de Coronado leads an expedition into what is now the southwestern United States

Spaniards rise against Napoléon's occupying army; the French are defeated in the Peninsula War

Bubonic plague begins to sweep through Europe, killing more than 25 million people

Bourbon dynasty takes Spanish throne after War of Spanish Succession

Historical Timeline

More than 350,000
Spaniards die in the
Spanish Civil War;
General Francisco
Franco's victory leads
to his long, brutal
dictatorship

Terrorist attacks on the
two World Trade Center
Towers in New York City
and on the Pentagon in
Washington, D.C., leave
thousands dead

Basque separatist
group ETA, which has
been fighting for an
independent Basque
region since 1959,
declares a cease-fire;
government plans
peace talks

Two U.S. astronauts
land on the moon

| 1931 | 1936-1939 | 1939-1945 | 1969 | 1975 | 2001 | 2004 | 2006 |

Spanish king forced to
leave throne and Spain
becomes a republic

Terrorists linked to
al-Qaeda bomb
rush-hour trains
in Madrid, killing
nearly 200 people;
Socialists win
general election

World War II

Juan Carlos de Borbón
becomes king after
Franco dies; Spain forms
constitutional monarchy

Glossary

abolished | when the use or effect of something has been ended or destroyed

autonomous | in a government, to be independent and subject to its own laws only

dictatorship | government by a ruler who took complete control of a country, often unjustly

discrimination | treating people unfairly because of their race, religion, sex, or age

elective | related to courses that students can choose to take but are not required

gored | to be pierced or wounded with something sharp, such as a bull's horn

gross domestic product (GDP) | the total value of all goods and services produced in a country

prominent | widely or popularly known; leading

resurrection | to rise from the dead

vocational | a skill or trade pursued as a career

Additional Resources

IN THE LIBRARY

Bader, Philip. *Spain*. Vero Beach, Fla.:
    Rourke Book Co., 2001.

Champion, Neil. *Spain*. New York: Facts
    on File, 2005.

Taus-Bolstad, Stacy. *Spain in Pictures*.
    Minneapolis: Lerner Publications, 2004.

Townsend, Sue, and Caroline Young. *Spain*.
    Chicago: Heinemann Library, 2003.

Wightwick, Jane. *Spanish Phrase Book*. New
    York: Passport Books, 2001.

ON THE WEB

For more information on this topic, use
FactHound.

1. Go to www.facthound.com
2. Type in this book ID: 0756524466
3. Click on the *Fetch It* button.

Look for more Global Connections books.

Teens in Australia
Teens in Brazil
Teens in China
Teens in France
Teens in India
Teens in Israel
Teens in Japan

Teens in Kenya
Teens in Mexico
Teens in Russia
Teens in Saudi Arabia
Teens in Venezuela
Teens in Vietnam

Source Notes

Page 21, column 2, line 6: Laurie M. Scott. "Back to School Around the World." *The Christian Science Monitor*. 4 Sept. 2001. 23 June 2006. www.csmonitor.com/2001/0904/p13s1-lekt.html

Page 37, column 2, line 25: *Ibid.*

Page 41, column 1, line 18: Todd Novak. "Sabin Biskarrelogorra Bravo: Basque Teenager, and My Friend." Googolplex. 30 Nov. 2006. http://googolplex.cuna.org/12433/cnote/story.html?doc_id=594

Page 45, sidebar, line 10: Daniel Ochoa de Olza. "The Thin Ban." *USA Today*. 15 Sept. 2006. 15 Sept. 2006.

Page 76, column 2, line 10: Adella Gooch. "Problems of Female Matador." *The Tribune*. 5 June 1999. 30 Nov. 2006. www.tribuneindia.com/1999/99jun05/spr-trib.htm#3

Pages 84–85, At a Glance: United States. Central Intelligence Agency. *The World Factbook—Spain*. 14 Nov. 2006. 21 Nov. 2006. www.cia.gov/cia/publications/factbook/geos/sp.html

Select Bibliography

"Education at a Glance 2004." *OECD Education*. 21 Nov. 2006. www.oecd.org/dataoecd/51/21/37392840.pdf

"Education & Schooling in Spain." *AngloINFO Costa Blanca (Spain)*. 15 Aug. 2006. http://costablanca.angloinfo.com/countries/spain/schooling.asp

Globalis. *Spain*. 21 Nov. 2006. http://globalis.gvu.unu.edu/country.cfm?country=ES

Gooch, Adella. "Probelms of Female Matador." *The Tribune*. 5 June 1999. 30 Nov. 2006. www.tribuneindia.com/1999/99jun05/spr-trib.htm#3

Graff, Marie Louise. *Culture Shock! Spain*. Portland, Ore.: Graphic Arts Center, 1997.

Hampshire, David. *Living and Working in Spain: A Survival Handbook*. London: Survival Books, 2004.

Nash, Elizabeth. *Madrid: A Cultural and Literary Companion*. New York: Interlink Books, 2001.

Novak, Todd. "Sabin Biskarrelogorra Bravo: Basque Teenager, and My Friend." Googolplex. 30 Nov. 2006. http://googolplex.cuna.org/12433/cnote/story.html?doc_id=594

Ochoa de Olza, Daniel. "The Thin Ban." *USA Today*. 15 Sept. 2006.

Oxfam Cool Planet On the Line—Virtual Journey Through Spain. *Daily Life*. 21 Nov. 2006. www.oxfam.org.uk/coolplanet/ontheline/explore/journey/spain/daylife1.htm

Porter, Darwin, and Danforth Prince. *Frommer's Spain 2006*. Hoboken, N.J.: Wiley, 2005.

Rodgers, Eamonn, ed. *Encyclopedia of Contemporary Spanish Culture*. London: Routledge, 1999.

Scott, Laurie M. "Back to School Around the World." *The Christian Science Monitor*. 4 Sept. 2001. 23 June 2006. www.csmonitor.com/2001/0904/p13s1-lekt.html

St. Jorre, John de. *Traveler's Companion: Spain*. Old Saybrook, Conn.: 1998.

United States. Central Intelligence Agency. *The World Factbook—Spain*. 14 Nov. 2006. 21 Nov. 2006. www.cia.gov/cia/publications/factbook/geos/sp.html

Index

About the Author
Jason Skog

Jason Skog is a writer who lives in Brooklyn, New York, with his wife and son. He worked as a newspaper reporter for 12 years, covering education, courts, police, government and youth issues. His work has appeared in magazines and newspapers. This is his fourth book for young readers.

About the Content Adviser
Maria del Mar Gomez, M.S.

We were fortunate to have Maria del Mar Gomez, a published author, serve as our content adviser for *Teens in Spain*. As she reviewed the manuscript, she was living in Madrid and working as an assistant professor of Spanish literature and cultures at New York University in Madrid. In September 2006, Maria del Mar Gomez moved from Spain to New York to study for her doctorate at New York University.